Body Language

*How to Read and Analyze People &
the Science of Human Psychology*

Table of Contents

Introduction

I want to thank you and congratulate you for purchasing the book, *"Body Language: How to Read and Analyze People & the Science of Human Psychology"*.

This book has actionable information on how to read an analyze people and the science of human psychology.

The ability to read and analyze another person's true intentions, determine the person's personality and find out what the person is truly thinking based on his or her words and body language is a truly remarkable skill to have. Think about it; the ability to attune yourself to a person's true intentions can greatly aid your desire to build meaningful bonds, form strong relationships, and even make more informed, effective decisions.

If you are wondering why you should develop this body language skill and the ability to read people like a book, here is the answer: because it can help you empathize and ascertain how others truly feel, and in a professional capacity, when you can accurately connect with the people around you, you appear as an effective leader.

Human beings are complex creatures.

Sometimes the words we use to communicate can hold a much deeper meaning, more than we may be willing to let on. While our words may say one thing, our body language can tell an entirely different story, a more *honest and accurate* story, because as adept as we may be at using words to conceal the truth, our bodies make terrible liars. Don't let others fool you with their body language.

And lucky for you, the information you are about to uncover in this book is going to help you learn how to decipher body language, look for telltale clues that tell you what a person really feels, build connections, and identify emotions and read expression in a more effective manner.

Let's get started.

Thanks again for purchasing this book. I hope you enjoy it!

Chapter 1: The Power of Words

"By words we learn thoughts, and by thoughts we learn life."

Jean Baptiste Girard

How amazing is it that a few simple words can dramatically change a situation? The words a person chooses to use can give great insight into what the person feels, thinks, and perceives. In simpler terms, words can help you understand someone's deepest thoughts and emotions. Through learning how to decipher the messages hidden within those words, we learn how to read another person.

How Powerful Are Words Anyway?

They say if you want to know someone, you should look into the person's eyes: the eyes are the window to a person's soul. If that is the case, then words are the windows into a person's mind. The words someone chooses to speak represent what the said person is thinking.

To connect with someone, you need to be able to understand where the person is coming from and what he or she is trying to say. Listening or reading the words spoken by another can be helpful tools in deciphering and predicting what the person's next move might be—it can even clue you in on the person's personality.

Humans communicate verbally; we describe this form of communication quite simply as *verbal communication*. Verbal communication is how we best channel and express our ideas, concepts, and desires. Words offer more than powerful insights into the mind of a person. They are also a very valuable tool in the teaching and learning process.

When used in tandem with forms of nonverbal communication, it is possible to convey messages that pack a powerful punch, but only to someone who knows how to read nonverbal communication.

Communication, language, and words are all an important part of the human experience. It is how we teach, how we learn, how we inquire, inform, discuss, argue, build bonds and form relationships.

Words are powerful because they help you, the listener, gain valuable insights that you can then use to make educated guesses, predict, or form your own hypothesis about another individual. For example, if someone were to say to you *"I was in a hurry,"* by noticing and observing the key words in the sentence, in this case "hurry," you will be able to deduce that this person wanted to get somewhere very quickly and may have been rushing to do so.

This sentence conveys a sense of urgency, and from it, you could make an educated guess that wherever the person was rushing was important. You could take that even further by hypothesizing that this individual could be someone who likes deadlines, does not like to miss appointments, and is conscientious and respectful of other people's time, all that from picking up on the key word: *hurry.*

Proven Strategies for Reading People through the Words They Use

While words certainly carry a power of their own, there is something else even more powerful: body language, in this respect, the ability to decipher the messages hidden behind a person's subtle gestures and nuances. To read someone effectively, you will have to look beyond just what the person is saying and observe the way he or she is saying it too.

Decipher the hidden messages behind the words someone chooses to use is easy enough; you just need to keep your ears open to the key words and phrases within each sentence. Knowing how to read beyond words on the other hand, is where the next three strategies are going to come in handy.

Strategy #1: Reading the Lips

You are about to discover how to read hidden body language clues through someone's *lip movement*. Understanding these cues will give you an even deeper insight into what someone is truly trying to convey.

When combined with the words someone chooses to use in speech, the position of a person's lips, *pouted, pursed, thin-lipped smile or lop-sided grin*, can tell a very powerful story about what a person is thinking and feeling. This is why body language is even more powerful than words: because it subconsciously reflects a person's *true feelings*, sometimes without the person realizing how he or she is using the body to communicate. For example, a person could say, "I *am happy*," and while the keyword in that phrase is "happy," if the person says it while his or her lips are tense and pursed, you will immediately know that there may be more to the story than what the person is choosing to reveal.

Strategy #2: Reading Facial Expressions

Beyond the face, someone's entire facial expression will tell you the real story of what the said person is really thinking. When someone says, "*I am happy for Bob and the promotion he got,*" but you notice a little sneer of the lips, a downward curve of the person's mouth as he or she says it, or a slight frown between the brows, you will immediately know that those may not be the person's true feelings at all.

The subconscious movements of a person's lips and mouth area, along with their words, are the two tools you need to use to read people successfully. This is why it is so important to notice *both* aspects, because oftentimes, a person's words do not necessarily match up to what the person is truly feeling.

When in conversation, notice your counterpart's overall facial expressions as he or she speaks and see if the words the person chooses to use match up to what his or her face is telling you.

Strategy #3: Notice the Rest of Their Body

What else is their body doing as they speak to you? If the person you are talking to says, *"Yeah, sure that sounds great,"* what is the rest of their body doing while the person says this sentence? You have attuned the keyword "great," but now you will need to dig a little deeper to see if the person is telling you what you want to hear.

Are the person's arms relaxed by the side of the body or crossed tensely in front of his or her chest? If it is the latter, it is probably a safe bet to say that "great" is not how the person truly feels about your proposal. Let's take the discussion further by discussing how to read body language like a pro.

Chapter 2: How to Read Body Language like A Pro

We tend to focus more on what a person says. The words and actions a person chooses to use to communicate often take center stage and body language plays second fiddle and in most cases, we pay very little attention to it.

Part of the reason for this is a misconception that words are our primary mode of communication; they are not. In fact, <u>Professor Mehrabian once claimed that nonverbal communications make up more than 93% of our communications</u>. Body language is *precisely what* we should be noticing the most.

Learning to communicate well verbally is a good skill to have, but to become a truly *effective communicator*, you will have to take your communication skills to the next level by learning to understand what people are *not saying* to you.

The Basics of Body Language

When it comes to learning how to read body language, the main goal is trying to determine if the person in front of you is being genuine. Body language clues are extremely crucial when trying to decipher someone's innermost thoughts, personality, and even intentions. In many ways, body language teaches you to become a human lie detector. Humans can be great liars, but while we may have been able to trick our mind into saying words we do not mean, we cannot trick our body into executing the lie perfectly.

Being able to read body language is an excellent skill to have in situations such as job interviews, when you are trying to solve a crime or resolve conflict. Being able to see beneath the surface into what is really going on inside someone's mind will help you make better, more informed decisions.

What makes body language so tricky a skill to master is the need to decipher body language cues within the right context. For example, when a person crosses his or her arms in front of the chest, you could construe that as negative body language, perhaps an indicator that the person is not happy to be here. However, depending on the context, it could also mean that the person is feeling cold, uncomfortable, or frustrated. Not accounting for the context of a situation can lead to misreading of body language cues and a wrong conclusion.

Most people generally display a few categories of body language:

1. **Dominant:** Dominant body language comes into play when someone wants to be in command. The most standout cue for this category of body language is someone standing tall, with his or her chest puffed out.

2. **Attentive:** This shows someone's interest and engagement with the conversation or situation.

3. **Bored:** A common representation of this body language is the lack of eye contact and constant yawning.

4. **Aggressive:** An aggressive person will display threatening body language cues.

5. **Defensive:** A defensive person will look as if he or she is protecting or withholding information.

6. **Closed Off:** You can recognize a closed off person by noticing if he or she is shutting you off by crossing his or her arms and guardedly standing farther away from you.

7. **Open:** This body language is friendly and welcoming.

8. **Emotional:** We normally display this body language when we feel heavily influenced current feelings and usually have changing moods.

Foolproof Techniques for Boosting Your Body Language Reading Skills

If you know just what to look for, body language can provide you with invaluable information. The following strategies will teach you how read someone's body language like a pro.

Strategy #4: The eyes speak volumes

Pay close attention to someone's eyes. If someone is avoiding eye contact, there is a strong possibility that he or she is either uncomfortable, disinterested, nervous or bored. If the person's pupils appear dilated, it is safe to say that the said person is comfortable and perhaps excited or even likes you.

If they person is blinking far too much (in an unnatural way), there is a strong possibility they the person is not being entirely honest with you. If the person looks to the left, he or she is trying to recall a genuine memory, and if to the right, it could be a sign that the person trying to make something up.

Strategy #5: Read the face

People will try to conceal and mask their facial expressions to the best of their ability. Sometimes though, their efforts are not good enough and the body has a way of giving off little telltale signs about what someone is truly thinking. Look for the subtle cues in someone's facial expressions.

A genuine smile is the easiest to read; it usually reaches a person's eyes. A fake smile on the other hand, looks stiff, tense, and off-putting. A half-smile on the other hand, could indicate that the person is uncomfortable or unsure. A tight-lipped smile is a sign of displeasure.

Strategy #6: Read the jaw and especially note the jaw clench

The next time you are talking to someone, take a quick look at the person's jaw. Does it appear clenched or relaxed? If you notice a little tension in the neck muscles, the person is giving off signs that he or she is experiencing a considerable amount of discomfort even when what the person says is not conveying that. If you notice these subtle signs, perhaps it might be best to postpone the conversation to another time or suggest moving it to a different location.

Strategy #7: Watch out for proximity

How close someone chooses to stand or sit next to you is a signal about how the person feels about you. If a person stands close to you in a relaxed, comfortable manner, it indicates that the person likes you and finds it easy to form rapport. However, if a person moves further away from you, it means the opposite. This is an example of where you need to consider context because in some cultures, people prefer to maintain a certain distance when interacting with each other and in such cases, proximity may not necessarily be a correct indicator about how they feel.

Strategy #8: Notice Mirroring

This is one of the very few instances where copying is perhaps a good thing. When someone mirrors your body movements, the person is subconsciously communicating liking you and having bonded enough to feel comfortable in your presence. When having conversations, you *want* people to mirror you because it means they are receptive to what you are saying and the conversation is going well.

Strategy #9: Notice the Palms

The palms of a person's hands can be very telling too. When a person's palms are open, it is an indication of honesty and a way of subconsciously communicating the lack of a threat. Have you noticed how people always put their hands up and palms facing outward as a sign of surrender?

Strategy #10: Happy feet

If someone likes you and is comfortable being around you, you will notice that the person's toes point inwards and face your direction.

With all we've learned in mind, we will now move on to discuss how to analyze people's behaviors.

Chapter 3: Building Connections by Reading Behavior

To understand and build better connections with the people around you, you first need to understand yourself. If you lack the necessary self-awareness to begin understanding why you do or say the things you do, how can you begin to understand someone else's intentions and where the person is coming from?

Self-awareness is a challenging skill to master. Understanding ourselves means we must be able to see both the good and the bad within us, to acknowledge our strengths and our flaws. For many, acknowledging flaws is the most difficult part of the process. Nobody likes to admit the faults that need work. Pride and ego get in the way, and that is why many people suffer from denial, completely blind to their own faults.

If you hope to build meaningful relationships with the people around you, you must overcome this trait. When you understand yourself, you become better able to empathize with others and see things from their perspective.

To start learning how to understand yourself (and others) better, take a look at the list below:

- Understand your desires and interests

- Acknowledge your needs and wants

- Find your passion

- Identify your emotions

- Be aware of your thoughts

- Appreciate the relationships you have

- Make a list of your skills, knowledge, and expertise

When you dig a little deeper into yourself and realize that certain qualities could be driving your thoughts, emotions and decisions, you will start to understand that these same circumstances could be driving the thoughts and decisions of others too. When you can better empathize and understand the people around you, it equips you with the skills and knowledge you need to form deeper, more meaningful relationships. Also, not trying to portray yourself as someone you are not helps establish trust.

Power-packed Tips to Read Other People's Behavior to Develop More Rewarding Interpersonal Relationships

Building trust is the foundation upon which you are going to start building more rewarding, interpersonal relationships with the people around you. In addition to deciphering what their body language is telling you, you have to present your intentions through your own body language.

To build strong relationships, you have to make other people feel comfortable enough to be around you, and even like you enough so you both have a mutual interest to form a strong, rewarding, interpersonal relationship with each other. If you are reading someone, you can bet that on some level, the person is also reading you too. For effective relationships to happen, both parties must like and trust each other enough to want to pursue the relationship.

If the other person is exhibiting signs of interest in forming a

17

strong rapport or relationship with you, here is what you can do to strengthen that bond for a more positive outcome:

Strategy #11: Relaxed Body Posture

You are not just looking for this sign in the other person; you have to exhibit a relaxed body posture of your own to make the other person feel comfortable. Avoid crossing your arms in front of your body, and make sure nothing in your body feels tense or stressed.

Strategy #12: Smiling and Nodding

If the person is doing this in a natural manner as you engage in conversation, you will know that the person is listening to you attentively and he or she likes you enough to be fully attentive. When the person takes his or her turn talking, exhibit the same behavior. To strengthen that mutual bond and likeness between the two of you, listen genuinely, attentively, and respond appropriately by nodding at the right moments. Remember not to overdo it though; you do not want to seem like you are trying too hard.

Strategy #13: Avoid Barriers

It is best if there are no barriers between you and the other person. A barrier could be anything from a table that is in the middle or sitting behind a desk at the office. It may not seem like a big deal, but these physical barriers could create subconscious barriers between you and the other person. Positioning yourself behind an object or a barrier is an example of a closed-off and unwelcoming body language.

Strategy #14: The Tilt of the Head

If you observe the person you are in a conversation with tilting his or her head ever so slightly as you speak, this is the person's body way of letting you know that the person is interested, trust, and approve of you. It means you are creating rapport.

If you observe Former President Barack Obama at some of his political debates, you will note that Mr. Obama often tilts his head to the side, indicating that he understood where his political opponents were coming from. He was also showing them that he was willing to listen without subconsciously resisting the points they were trying to make. If the person you are talking to exhibits this behavior when you are speaking, returning the favor when it is the person's turn to talk will strengthen that mutual bond and respect.

Strategy #15: Be Respectful

The biggest key to building rewarding, interpersonal relationships is to have mutual respect. Without respect, it is impossible for a strong bond to form. Avoid negative body language and condescending words or language that could indicate a lack of respect. Always be respectful with both your words and your body language, even if you happen to disagree with what the person is saying in that moment.

Strategy #16: Leaning Forward

Lean forwards especially when you are sitting down and having a discussion. When someone leans forward during a conversation, it denotes keen interest and attentive, and that the person likes and trusts you enough to be in close proximity to you. Reciprocating the gesture by leaning forward when the person is talking will let him or her know that the feeling is mutual.

With that in mind, our focus now will move to emotions.

Chapter 4: How to Read and Identify Emotions

Human emotions remain the driving force of many of the things we say, think, and do. Emotions can be a very powerful, volatile force within us that many of us sometimes have difficulty trying to control. When a person has learnt how to master not just their emotions, but also the ability to influence the emotions of others around him or her, it indicates that the person possess a high level of emotional intelligence.

The most telling indicator of a person's emotions is in the person's facial expressions. Sometimes those emotions cart over into other aspects of the body, but facial expressions remain the primary indicator.

To be able to identify someone's emotions, look towards his or her facial expressions as your first starting point. As adults, we often try to conceal our emotions as best as we can, especially within a professional environment, which is why it is important to look towards someone's body language as an indicator of the emotion the person may be experiencing.

Humans can experience a myriad of emotions, everything from stress, anger, happiness, joy, jubilation, exhilaration, enthusiasm and more. These emotions often have as accompaniment very telling signs given off by our bodies. Once you know what to look out for, you be able to identify a person's emotions.

When attempting to identify a person's emotions, there are few key indicators you want to look out for besides their facial expression:

- Their tone of voice

- Mannerisms

- Demeanor

- General behavior

- Observing a person's general physical health (emotions, when experienced in an extreme state, can affect our physical wellbeing)

Strategy #17: Signs of Anger

Quite possibly the easiest emotion to identify, anger has very telling body language. A deep frown, eyebrows pulled together fiercely, lips tight and thin, fists balled together, tense shoulders, nostrils flared, clenched jaw and muscles are all signs that exhibit anger as the current emotion a person is experiencing.

Strategy #18: Signs of Fear

Fear is our most primal emotions that evokes the fight or flight response. This emotion is also easy to identify because the person's body language will usually be a dead giveaway.

When someone is experiencing fear, his or her facial expression embodies this. The person's eyes widen, the fright becomes clearly visible on the person's face, the mouth is likely to open in either fear or shock, the lips could tremble, nostrils flared, and the person could, in some cases, break out in cold sweats (these beads of sweat normally first appear on the forehead).

Strategy #19: Signs of Deception

Humans may be adept at being deceptive with their words, but the human body makes for a very terrible liar. Not all lies have the intent of deceiving you. For example, when someone says, *"Yeah, I'm fine, don't worry about it'* and he or she is *not* fine, it could be the person's way of preventing you from asking more questions because the said individual does not necessarily feel like talking about it just yet. To sport when a person is being deceptive, you need to analyze the person's mannerisms and gestures after you have asked a question.

When someone is being deceptive, he or she usually sidesteps a question by giving long explanations or answers without actually addressing the issue. If you suspect someone is not being entirely honest with you, observe his or her mannerism for telling body language clues that accompany deception.

A deceptive person will touch his or her face or nose, or even cover his or her mouth or face because this is another subconscious way of hiding a lie. The stress of deception can also cause the skin to turn cold and start itching or even flush. Especially notice when someone suddenly scratch his or her ears or nose. Profuse sweating and avoiding eye contact are also telling signs of dishonesty even though verbally, they may be saying everything that they think you want to hear.

Strategy #20: Signs of Enthusiasm and Happiness

When a person is exhibiting signs of enthusiasm, he or she tends to nod and gesture a lot. If you look at people who are passionate about the topics they are talking about, you will notice that they tend to gesture a lot with their arms. They speak animatedly and gesture with their arms to emphasize the points that they are making. When a person is enthusiastic and happy about something, you will notice a lot of smiling as the person expresses his or her point.

Strategy #21: Signs of Unhappiness

Unhappiness can be a strong, difficult to hide emotion. When an unhappy person is in a conversation with you, you will notice that the person's upper body and feet shall appear positioned away from you, signaling the person's inner desire to end the conversation because his or her mind is on something else. The person could also display closed-off body language, arms crossed in front of their chest, shoulders hunched, and gaze downward, indicating their feelings of unhappiness.

Let's touch on emotional intelligence, as it is a very important part of reading people's emotions.

Improving Your Emotional Intelligence

Besides using the body language indicators above to help you identify some primary emotions we experience, another thing you could do is to consider developing your emotional intelligence. By teaching yourself how to identify and recognize emotions (not just in others, but also in yourself), you will be able to engage with an emotional person on a much deeper, personal level.

Because you can better empathize and understand where someone is coming from, you will be able to connect with someone even when the person is in an emotional state.

When you combine emotional intelligence with your ability to discern what a person is not saying, you will be able to grasp the important messages a lot better. This will then lead to you responding appropriately and making better, informed decisions because when you learn to observe more than just what you see on the surface, you can assess the situation and the person before you on a much deeper level.

To take your knowledge of how to read body language a notch higher, the next chapter will focus on how to read expressions, hand gestures and leg movements.

Chapter 5: How to Read Expressions, Hand Gestures, and Leg Movements

It is immensely intriguing how the body can tell a story entirely on its own without us even noticing it. This is what makes reading body language such an exciting skill to have. When you learn the art of reading body language, you become a detective that is trying to uncover the truth that people try to hide, revealing the things that they will not ever say aloud with their words.

We tend to focus so much on what the person is trying to say that we sometimes forget to watch out for how the person uses his or her body language specifically in three selected areas that tell the loudest story.

This is what we are going to uncover in our final chapter.

How to Read Expressions

By this point, it is safe to say that to know a person's true intentions, you are going to have to become an expert at reading the person's facial expressions. This is more than recognizing familiar facial expressions though. You also need to be able to *understand* what the person is trying to say through those expressions, the message the person is trying to communicate. Reading facial expressions only has one technique to it: *be carefully observant of a person's face.* That is all you need to do: focus on the face.

Charles Darwin was the first put forth the notion that certain facial expressions associated with certain emotions were universal. He proposed this idea back in 1872, and sometime in the 1960s, Silvan Tomkins confirmed through a study that facial expressions are indeed reliably associated with certain emotional states that the human body experiences.

While common emotions such as fear, anger, sadness, and happiness are easy enough to identify because the facial expressions are universal, there is another element to reading facial expressions: *macro expression.*

A macro expression usually lasts about four or five seconds. Macro expressions also occur only when a person is entirely comfortable in the immediate surroundings and the people in that environment. Macro expressions occur when a person makes a certain facial expressions used to accompany a particular emotion the person may be feeling. These expressions last much longer on our faces because out of comfort, we do not feel the need to conceal our true emotions.

A macro expression is what you might call a shorter version of a person's emotional facial expression. Because this expression can take place in the blink of an eye, if you are not watching out for it, you are likely to miss it. Keep a close eye out for these expressions the next time you are in a conversation with someone.

NOTE: As you continue developing your facial reading expertise, keep in mind that by doing so, you are only creating a hypothesis of what the person may be feeling. Facial expressions do not necessarily confirm what a person is feeling or what is causing the person to feel that emotion (remember the context scenario).

Remember that facial expressions are only an indication of the emotion someone may be experiencing in that moment. Always ask, and never assume. Just because someone is frowning does not automatically mean that the person is without a doubt angry. Use that as a prompt and gently ask the person if he or she is feeling all right.

How to Read Hand Gestures

Hand gesturing is a natural part of us. We use it without even thinking twice about it, sometimes a little bit too much when we are excited or extremely emotional. Hand gestures are just as much a part of our communication process as our words.

When used correctly, gesturing makes people take notice of what you are trying to say, especially when you accompany those gestures correctly with the words you are trying to emphasize. Hand gestures reveal hidden clues about what a person may be thinking or feeling.

Here is how to decipher some of the most commonly used hand gestures:

- **Brow Rubbing:** This gesture indicates that a person could be worried or doubtful.

- **Scratching the Head:** Scratching the head could indicate a person who is in deep thought or trying to solve a problem; depending on the context, it could also indicate confusion.

- **Running Fingers through Hair:** Closely related to head scratching, this is often an indication that a person is feeling uncertain or unsure or trying to think of something.

- **Eye Rubbing:** An indication that a person is feeling fatigued.

- **Index Finger on Temple:** This gesture indicates that a person could be thinking of something. Sometimes, it is also an indication of a person in critical thoughts.

- **Nose Touching:** Generally associated with being an indication that a person is lying. If casually done, it could be an indication that the person feels pressured about something.

- **Covering of the Mouth:** If this gesture appears when a person is listening to someone else, it is an indication that the listener does not necessarily believe the speaker. If someone does this *while* talking, it could be an indication of dishonesty. Sometimes, it is also an indication that a person is thinking hard about something

- **Lip Holding:** This is often an indication that a person is feeling greedy.

- **Putting Fingers in the Mouth:** This gesture indicate that a person may need further reassurance before making a decision.

- **Stroking of the Chin:** This gesture normally indicates that a person is thinking.

- **Ear Rubbing:** Rubbing behind the ear is an indication that a person is afraid of being misunderstood, or that he or she is afraid of not understanding.

- **Earlobe Touching:** Touching the earlobe is an indication that a person is looking for comfort.

- **Open Palms or Outstretched Arms:** An indication of openness, trustworthiness, and acceptance.

- **Palms Down:** Palms down normally indicates confidence and is sometimes a sign of rigidness and a sense of authority.

- **Hands behind the Back:** Hand behind the back is an indication of confidence—most commonly used by men.

- **Finger Pointing:** This gesture is an indication that a person is feeling authoritative. At other time, it serves as an indication of aggressive or angry emotions.

How to Read Leg Movements

Who would have thought the position of a person's legs could reveal so much about what a person is thinking and feeling. Most of the time, we focus so much on what the upper body language of a person communicates that we forget about the legs and the story they tell.

Here are some of the hidden messages that a person could be revealing with his or her leg movements:

- **Sitting Down, Legs Slightly Apart:** This indicates that the person is feeling both relaxed and comfortable.

- **Legs Crossed While Standing:** This indicates that the person could be feeling shy. We can consider it a submissive stance or an indication that a person does not feel entirely comfortable in specific surroundings or the company.

- **Legs Crossed and Relaxed While Sitting:** A very common gesture in many Asian and European cultures— 70% of people generally cross their left leg over their right. However, when accompanied with arms crossed over the chest, this gesture can be an indication of an emotionally withdrawn or closed off person.

- **Sitting Down, Ankles Crossed:** An indication that the person is feeling fairly relaxed. If accompanied by clenched hands, this could be an indication that the person is feeling rigid or tense, or a signal of self-restraint.

- **Sitting Down, Ankles Crossed, and Tucked under Chair:** This gesture could indicate a person that is trying to hide his or her feelings of anxiety.

- **Sitting Down, Knees Pointed:** If the person's knees are pointing towards you, it is an indication that the person finds you interesting or that he or she likes you. If the knees point away from you, it is an indication of disinterest.

- **Standing, Leg Bouncing/Foot Tapping:** This gesture indicates that that the person could be feeling impatient.

- **Sitting, Leg Bouncing:** If a person is moving his or her legs up and down while sitting, it is an indication of impatience. Sometimes, depending on the context, the person could be bouncing his or her leg or tapping the foot when either relaxed or enjoying the environment (for example, if music is playing in the background).

- **Standing Parallel, Feet Close Together:** This is an indication that a person is displaying a neutral attitude—often considered a more formal standing position.

- **Standing, Legs Apart:** This is predominantly common among men. It indicates a person is firm and standing his ground. Often seen when a person is trying to display a sense of dominance.

- **Sitting, Figure Four Crossed Leg -** If accompanied by both hands clamped down on the crossed leg, it is an indication that the person could be someone who has a competitive, stubborn, or tough nature.

Conclusion

Thank you for making it to the end of this book!

I trust that reading the book has equipped you with the tools you need to read and understand the secret clues and messages that people tell with their body language. These skills will come in handy not just in everyday life as you try to form relationships with others, but also in your career as you use these skills to your advantage to give you the advantage you need to climb the career ladder.

As you become a master at deciphering the intricate world of communication through body language, you will connect better, empathize better, and reveal the hidden stories behind a person's true desire, thoughts, and intentions.

If you found the book valuable, can you recommend it to others? One way to do that is to post a review on Amazon.

Click here to leave a review for this book on Amazon!

Thank you and good luck!